# In C[illegible] Blood



Truman Capote

## TEACHER GUIDE

**NOTE:**

The trade book edition of the novel used to prepare this guide is found in the Novel Units catalog and on the Novel Units website. Using other editions may have varied page references.

Please note: We have assigned Interest Levels based on our knowledge of the themes and ideas of the books included in the Novel Units sets, however, please assess the appropriateness of this novel or trade book for the age level and maturity of your students prior to reading with them. You know your students best!

**ISBN 978-1-60878-732-6**



Printed in the United States of America.

**To order, contact your local school supply store, or:**

Toll-Free Fax: 877.716.7272
Phone: 888.650.4224
3901 Union Blvd., Suite 155
St. Louis, MO 63115

sales@novelunits.com

**novelunits.com**

# Table of Contents



# Skills and Strategies

**Critical Thinking**
Analyzing, inference, research, opinions, prediction

**Comprehension**
Plot development, compare/contrast, cause/effect

**Literary Elements**
Symbolism, imagery, metaphors, static/dynamic characters, conflict, irony, foreshadowing

**Vocabulary**
Definitions, application, synonyms/antonyms

**Writing**
Essays, poetry, news story, letter to the editor, synopsis

**Listening/Speaking**
Presentation, discussion, news report, book review, art analysis

**Across the Curriculum**
Literature—book review, author interview, New Journalism, François Villon; Social Studies—current events, religion, jury selection, capital punishment, subliminal messages, interview techniques; Art—cover art, photography, painting, collage, symbols

**Genre:** nonfiction, true crime

**Setting:** Holcomb, Garden City, and Kansas City, Kansas; Las Vegas, Nevada; various locations in Mexico and the Western United States

**Point of View:** third-person omniscient

**Themes:** fear, trust, suspicion, regret, good versus evil, loss of innocence, class structure, distortion of self-image, effects of a troubled childhood, destruction of the family unit

**Conflict:** person vs. society, person vs. self, person vs. person

**Style:** investigative true account documenting a multiple murder and the subsequent trial; one of the first examples of "New Journalism"

**Tone:** solemn, factual, intimate

**Date of First Publication:** 1965

## Summary

Herbert Clutter and his family are prosperous, though humble, members of the Holcomb, Kansas community. One night in November 1959, four members of the Clutter family are bound and murdered in their home by Perry Smith and Dick Hickock. While the actual murders are not described until later in the book, Capote thoroughly examines the lives of the Clutters and the convicted murderers prior to that fateful night. Capote explores the murder investigation, the community's response, and the murderers' flight across the country and into Mexico. Smith and Hickock's relationship begins to deteriorate, and they return to the United States to commit more crimes. Meanwhile, they attempt to avoid the police and forget about the Clutter murders. Smith and Hickock are eventually caught when they return to Las Vegas and are recognized by the authorities. Through the duration of the book, Capote details Smith and Hickock's childhoods, their reasons for killing the Clutter family, and their time on Death Row. Capote also relates the solemn yet hopeful lives of those in the Holcomb community as they attempt to return to normal following the capture and execution of Smith and Hickock.

## About the Author

Truman Capote (1924–1984), born Truman Streckfus Persons, was an American author best known for his early short stories and essays, many of which were published in the most respected literary magazines of the time, such as *The Atlantic Monthly*, *Harper's Bazaar*, and *The New Yorker*. His success led to a career as a novelist, and his novella *Breakfast at Tiffany's* inspired fellow author Norman Mailer to call Capote "the most perfect writer of my generation." The novella was the basis for the 1961 film of the same name, starring Audrey Hepburn. After becoming fascinated with a news brief in *The New York Times* that relayed the initial story of the Clutter murders in Kansas, Capote set out for Holcomb with his friend Harper Lee (who would later write the literary classic *To Kill a Mockingbird*). The two interviewed many of those involved with the case (some numerous times) during the search for the killers and the subsequent trial. Capote is also notorious for developing a close relationship with Perry Smith and Dick Hickock prior to their executions—these relationships are what helped Capote provide such a detailed description of the killers' lives before and after the murder. *In Cold Blood* became a wildly popular literary landmark and helped usher in "New Journalism," a style of nonfiction writing that documents current events by blending journalistic intention with creative, literary style. Capote continued to write other books and maintained his celebrity status by making numerous television appearances. During the final years of his life, many of Capote's celebrity relationships were strained due to his "tell-all" publications detailing the lives of those in high society. Capote's mental and physical deterioration, including seizures and hallucinations, left him unable to finish much of his later writings. He died in Los Angeles from liver cancer at age 59. His writing style was both praised and criticized during his lifetime, and his openness about his homosexuality also created controversy during a period when such lifestyles were hidden from and frowned upon by the general public. Since Capote's death, *In Cold Blood* has remained one of the most renowned books in American literature, and many movies, including *Capote* (2005), were based on his life and this seminal work.

## Characters

**Note:** There are many minor characters throughout the book who affect the plot. The major characters are listed below.

**Perry Smith:** 31 years old at the time of the crime; a quiet, hypersensitive individual who suffered an abusive childhood, which led to an array of psychological imbalances; served in the military but displayed antisocial and violent tendencies; has noticeably short, thin legs as a result of an injury suffered in a motorcycle accident, an injury which causes him chronic pain; It is assumed that Perry was the one who actually shot and killed four members of the Clutter family.

**Richard "Dick" Hickock:** 28 years old at the time of the crime; a quick-talking criminal known for writing bad checks, theft, and predatory sexual advances upon female adolescents; was an athlete and an adept mechanic as a young man; has a disfigured face as a result of a car accident; displays psychological imbalances and was eager to kill the Clutter family for their alleged money; the driving force behind the crime

**Herbert "Herb" Clutter:** a 48-year-old farmer of modest wealth; well-liked in Holcomb and Garden City; noted for being tall, strong, quiet, and a solemn Christian; He refused to hire any man who drank, and some believed that he hid money on his farm, though this was not the case.

**Bonnie Clutter:** Herb's 45-year-old wife; suffered from an anxiety disorder and spent most of her time resting indoors; Though well-liked, her condition prompted some gossip in town.

**Nancy Clutter:** Herb's 16-year-old daughter; adored by the community and referred to as "the town darling" (p. 7)

**Kenyon Clutter:** Herb's 15-year-old son; a tall boy who liked to hunt and tinker with inventions in the basement of the Clutter home

**Alvin Adams Dewey:** the 47-year-old Kansas Bureau of Investigation (KBI) lead investigator in the Clutter murder case; lived near Garden City, knew of Herb Clutter, and became obsessed with finding the murderers

**Harold Nye, Roy Church, and Clarence Duntz:** the three KBI agents working under Alvin Dewey who piece together the evidence that aided in the capture and conviction of Smith and Hickock



 

**Bobby Rupp:** Nancy's boyfriend; the last person to see the family alive; claimed he felt a strange sensation of being watched as he left the Clutter home the night they were murdered; is initially a suspect but is quickly dismissed

**Susan Kidwell:** Nancy's close friend; one of two girls who discovers the murdered family

**Tex John Smith:** Perry Smith's father; former rodeo rider; The two had a powerful love/hate relationship that had a detrimental impact on both Perry and his sister Fern.

**Floyd Wells:** former cellmate of Dick Hickock; used to work for Herb Clutter; tells Hickock that Clutter has a safe and keeps money hidden there; thinks Hickock is joking when the plan to kill Clutter is revealed; His testimony helps convict Hickock and Smith.

**Willie-Jay:** a chaplain's clerk whom Perry befriends; encourages Perry's creativity; Perry later questions this friendship when Willie-Jay tries to guide Perry toward Christianity and a wholesome life.

## Initiating Activities

Use one or more of the following to introduce the book.

1. Have students research the genre of "New Journalism." Have each student give a three-minute oral presentation on a "New Journalism" book or author, explaining how their selection had an effect upon our society and/or literature. Each student should also explain their thoughts on whether or not "New Journalism" is more journalistic or creative. Students can consult the "Acknowledgements" at the beginning of the book for more information.
2. In groups of two or three, have students examine both the photograph of Holcomb and the two close-up photos of the murderers' eyes on the cover of the book. Have members in each group explain what they think these images tell a reader before they open the book, as well as describe the symbolism and subliminal messages these photos create. Students can also research other subliminal messages in popular culture and present their findings.
3. Have students research the François Villon poem excerpted at the beginning of the book. After reading an English translation of the poem, each student should write a paragraph about what the excerpt means and how it might relate to the plot of *In Cold Blood*.
4. Divide the class into four or five groups to play "Word Survival." Using the Glossary on pages 36–40 of this guide, write a vocabulary word on the board and ask each group (one at a time) to supply either a synonym or an antonym for the word. Each group must rely on the groups' collective knowledge to "survive." Groups should continue to supply synonyms or antonyms for the chosen words until one group cannot answer. The group that cannot answer must have a member of their group sit out. Write another vocabulary word to start a new round. The last group with students remaining is the winner.



 

## Part I: The Last To See Them Alive
## Pages 1–37

Truman Capote introduces the reader to the Clutter family of Holcomb, Kansas, following them through the days before their murder and depicting their simple lifestyle. He presents the Clutters as representative of the wholesome 1950s American household. Life on the Clutters' farm consisted of hard work and simple pleasures, and the Clutters were respected and popular members of the community. Capote also introduces Perry Smith and Dick Hickock and leads the reader through the days before their crime. Capote describes the two men as self-obsessed dreamers who are excited about the crime they are about to commit. Dick is especially eager and cannot wait to kill the farmer and his family once they have robbed the Clutters' alleged secret safe. Perry and Dick purchase the supplies they think they will need to commit their crime and continue driving toward Holcomb.

**Vocabulary**

haphazard
melancholy
exploitation
impinged
disquiet
abstemious
despondent
ominous
mesmeric
pragmatic
enigma
reticent
ineffable
elocution
diminutive
vitality
austere
admonition
fastidious
truncated
itinerant
opulent
wanton

### Discussion Questions

1. How does Capote describe the town of Holcomb? Why might Holcomb be an attractive venue for criminals? *(Capote describes Holcomb as a "lonesome area" on the plains of western Kansas. The town itself is "an aimless congregation of buildings" [p. 3] divided by railroad tracks. Many of the older keystone businesses of the town are closed, and some, like the bank, are now apartment buildings. There are few actual businesses, and the school is perhaps the most significant building in town. The locals are "quite content to exist inside ordinary life" [p. 5]. Answers will vary. Students should note that law enforcement is scant, and no one would expect a terrible crime to occur in such a peaceful community so far removed from the troubles of the world. However, students should also note that since Holcomb is a small town, outsiders would be noticed easily.)*

2. According to Capote, what is ironic about the effect the Clutter murders had on Holcomb's tight-knit community? *(Capote alludes to the fact that after the crime, the members of this close community "viewed each other strangely, and as strangers" [p. 5], something they would never have expected since they have lived amongst each other for almost their entire lives. The crime makes them reassess who their neighbors are and question each other's motives.)*

3. How was Mr. Clutter viewed within the Holcomb community? What was the only "cause for disquiet" (p. 7) in his life? *(Mr. Clutter was not the wealthiest man in town, but he was "the community's most widely known citizen" [p. 6] who held positions on local church committees and farming organizations and was dedicated to hard work and his family. Mr. Clutter's only real worry was his wife's health. Holcomb residents were aware that Mrs. Clutter suffered "little spells" and had a nervous condition that kept her at home most days, unable to interact much with her friends in the community. She saw many doctors for treatment and hoped to return to her old self.)*

4. What two things might prohibit someone from approaching the Clutters' farm, and how might these things prove useless as a deterrent for criminals? *(Although the Clutters lived far from town and had no neighbors within a half mile, the Stoeckleins, who worked for Herb Clutter, lived in a small house less than 100 yards from the farm. The Stoekleins' proximity might have*



 

*deterred any prowlers, unless the person entered silently and in the dark. The Clutters also owned a dog named Teddy, who would alert the family if someone came near the house at night. However, Teddy cowered at the sight of guns.)*

5. What "worldly belongings" does Perry keep with him, and what might these items reveal about him? *(He keeps hundreds of maps from every state and all over the world, a cardboard suitcase, a guitar, and two boxes filled with books, more maps, songs, letters, and poems, all of which weighed "a quarter of a ton" [p. 14]. These items show that Perry has no permanent home and keeps his belongings with him as he travels. They also show that he has traveled extensively, that he values his past and his future more than the present, and that he is a bit of a loner. His guitar and poems show that he is creative, but the fact that he keeps his writings boxed up likely means that Perry is shy and insecure. However, he is proud enough to boast about how much he spent on the books and on shipping them around the country with him, defending himself from Dick's accusation that the boxes are filled with "junk.")*

6. In what ways does Perry seem self-obsessed? Are his dreams realistic or not? *(Answers will vary. Perry demonstrates that he is self-obsessed by lugging around a quarter ton of his belongings everywhere he goes, even though he could store these items somewhere. He also stops every time he sees a mirror or his reflection in a window and studies his face, going "into a trance" [p. 15] as he marvels at the many different expressions he can make. Perry's plans of going to Mexico to find treasure are based on movies, even though he says his father has taught him how to hunt for gold. He collects brochures and books about finding treasure and imagines himself living a simple, adventurous lifestyle without considering the difficulties such a life would present. He later imagines himself as a lounge singer in Las Vegas, where he plays guitar and sings to an adoring crowd. These fascinations most likely have little chance of coming true, and Perry may focus on them because his own life is depressing and uninteresting.)*

7. How do you think Truman Capote was able to recreate private conversations, such as Nancy's telephone conversations on pages 19–22 of the book and those between the Clutter family members? *(Answers will vary, but Capote likely interviewed anyone who spoke with the Clutters or overheard conversations and recreated them from details culled from those interviews. However, in New Journalism it is common for authors to fill in gaps with actions, conversations, and details that the author believes may have occurred based on what else they know about the people involved. Although Capote often denied that he wrote in the New Journalism style, the author's subjectivity plays a role in the telling of the Clutter murders, a common characteristic of this style.)*

8. What equipment did Dick have in his car when he picked up Perry outside the drugstore? How did he think these items would help them, and what can you infer from this? *(Dick had a 12-gauge pump-action shotgun, a flashlight, a fishing knife, leather gloves, and a hunting vest with extra shells. Dick believed it would appear the two men had been hunting, should they encounter anyone on their trip to the Clutter home or back. Answers will vary, but students might discuss how Dick probably planned to get messy while at the Clutters, as proven by his promise to Perry: "...we'll blast hair all over them walls" [p. 22]. Dick believed hunting would be a good excuse for their appearance following their visit to the Clutters.)*

9. What "projects" caused Mrs. Clutter despair, and why? How was she unlike her husband? *(Mrs. Clutter was dreading the planning and execution of two major upcoming projects: hosting Thanksgiving and planning her daughter Beverly's wedding. Both of these would require her to be social and make decisions, something she had "learned to dread" [p. 28]. She found situations where she had to make decisions "unendurable." Herb Clutter was capable and decisive, easily hosting gatherings, giving speeches, and entertaining guests when needed. Mrs. Clutter believed her husband to be a "joiner" and a "born leader," the social outlet and head of the family.)*

10. **Prediction:** Will Dick's refusal to wear stockings backfire? Why or why not?

### Supplementary Activities

1. Complete the Characterization chart on page 29 of this guide.
2. Truman Capote foreshadows the Clutters' fate in a few ways, offering statements by friends or observations about the Clutters' traits that hint at the tragedy to come. Find at least two of these veiled references, and explain in a paragraph for each how these facts help build suspense.

## Pages 38–74

Capote continues to explore the personal traits and histories of the Clutter family members, focusing on Kenyon Clutter and his relationships with the other members of his family. Capote recounts how an insurance agent stopped by the farm to discuss life insurance with Herb Clutter, and Bobby Rupp describes the last evening he spent with Nancy and the rest of the Clutter family. Capote also delves into Perry's criminal background and his interactions with Willie-Jay, a chaplain's clerk who is sympathetic and friendly to Perry. Willie-Jay offers some psychological insight into Perry's qualities. As Dick and Perry drove closer and closer to their destination, they discussed the plan and contended with their anxiety. The two approached the dark house shortly after Nancy went to bed. Capote then jumps ahead to the next morning, explaining how friends of the family, concerned that the Clutters were not ready for church, went to the farm and discovered the murders. The news quickly spread through the town, and rumors began to circulate about the killers and their whereabouts. Meanwhile, Dick and Perry had already returned home and promptly fallen asleep.

| Vocabulary |
|---|
| temperament |
| credulous |
| ruminations |
| intervene |
| repertoire |
| agoraphobic |
| anecdote |
| encumbered |
| languid |
| pacified |
| unassuming |
| varmints |

### Discussion Questions

1. Whom did Mr. Clutter meet with the day before he died, and why was this meeting both tragic and ironic? *(Herb met with Bob Johnson, an insurance agent from Garden City, to discuss life insurance. After much discussion and debate, Mr. Clutter agreed to purchase a sizeable life insurance policy. Sadly, this meeting occurred just hours before Mr. Clutter and three members of his family were murdered. The meeting was ironic because Mr. Johnson and Mr. Clutter both agreed that Herb was in great health and had a long life ahead of him.)*
2. Who is Willie-Jay? Explain his relationship with Perry. *(Willie-Jay is a chaplain's clerk at Kansas State Penitentiary who befriended Perry and tried to guide him toward a relationship with God. Willie-Jay believed Perry was "a poet, something rare and savable" [p. 42]. He believed Perry's only flaw was that he exhibited "*explosive emotional reaction out of all proportion to the occasion*" [p. 43], meaning that Perry has rage issues and must get them under control. Perry appreciated Willie-Jay's encouragement and feels the man is his "real and only friend" [p. 42]. Perry believes that Willie-Jay is the only person to have "ever recognized [his] worth" [p. 45], and he wishes to see Willie-Jay again.)*



 

3. What caused Perry to agree to "Dick's proposition" instead of following a better path? *(Dick sent Perry a letter explaining that he had a "perfect score" that he wanted Perry to be a part of, but Perry was already working at integrating himself back into society. Perry went to Kansas City to find Willie-Jay, but he unfortunately arrived a few hours too late. Willie-Jay had boarded a bus heading east that very afternoon to find a job, leaving behind no contact information. At this point, Perry felt his "choice was between Dick and nothing" [p. 45], so he agreed to meet with Dick and hear about his proposition.)*

4. Who is Bobby Rupp, and what was his impression of the last moments spent with Nancy Clutter? *(Bobby Rupp was Nancy's boyfriend. He lived just three miles away from the Clutters and was the last person in the Holcomb community to see the family alive. He spent the evening with the Clutters, watching TV and talking with them. After the Clutters were murdered, the police questioned Bobby. Bobby told them he is now certain that as he left the house in the late evening, "somebody must have been hiding there...just waiting for [him] to leave" [p. 52].)*

5. When Perry and Dick stopped at the gas station on their way to the Clutters' farm, what did Dick consider about his partner in crime? *(Dick wondered if he misjudged Perry's character and began to second-guess Perry's convictions. He reflected upon how he used to think Perry was "a good guy" but a little "stuck on himself," "sentimental," and quite "the dreamer" [p. 54]. He only thought of Perry as a "natural killer" who would be of some advantage to him [Dick] after hearing Perry's story about murdering the man in Las Vegas. Dick originally believed he had tricked Perry into committing the crime, but he soon began to feel as though he was the one who was tricked. He wondered if all of his careful planning would be wasted because Perry planned to back out, and he vowed not to let that happen.)*

6. Who was the last of the Clutter family to go to sleep on the night of the murders, and what was in this person's final diary entry? How was this diary entry helpful to the investigating agents? *(Nancy Clutter was the last to go to bed that night. After she set out her clothing for the next day [which is known because it was likely found that way by the police the next day], she wrote in her diary as she had done every night over the last four years. She wrote, "Jolene K. came over and I showed her how to make a cherry pie. Practiced with Roxie. Bobby here and we watched TV. Left at eleven" [p. 57]. Nancy's diary entry showed that Bobby was the last person Nancy saw before her death, verifying his story. It also gave police a time frame for when the murders occurred—sometime after 11 p.m.)*

7. Why did Susan Kidwell call the Clutter family? What did she and Nancy Ewalt discover when they entered the Clutter house? *(Susan called the Clutter house because Nancy Ewalt and her father came to tell Susan that no one answered the Clutters' door. Nancy Ewalt and Susan always accompanied the Clutters to church, so Susan called the house, but no one answered. Mr. Ewalt suggested they go back and try again. When the girls entered the house, they found no evidence that the Clutters had eaten breakfast and they saw Nancy Clutter's purse lying open on the kitchen floor. They went up to Nancy's room first and found her dead, after which they ran screaming from the house.)*

8. What did Sheriff Robinson, Larry Hendricks, and Clarence Ewalt discover in the Clutters' master bedroom, and what was significant about these discoveries? *(They found Mr. Clutter's billfold, which appeared to have been rifled through, on his bed. They also found Mr. Clutter's glasses on the bureau. Answers will vary. The men knew that [a] Mr. Clutter never carried cash in his billfold and [b] Mr. Clutter couldn't see a thing without his glasses. These discoveries told them that the murderers were looking for money [and were likely not local since everyone in Holcomb knew that Herb Clutter didn't carry cash] and that wherever Herb was, he was definitely not there by choice since he had left his glasses behind.)*

9. How did Sheriff Robinson, Larry Hendricks, and Clarence Ewalt find Herb Clutter, and what haunts Hendricks the most about this? *(They found Herb Clutter in the furnace room in the basement. His ankles were tied, but his hands were not, as if he had managed to pull his hands free from the restraints. His mouth was taped, and he had been shot. However, unlike any other member of the family, Mr. Clutter's throat had been cut. Beneath him lay a large cardboard box upon which was half a bloody footprint. The image that most haunts Hendricks is the piece of cord tied to the steampipe above Herb. This led him to wonder if Herb had been tortured, a thought that disturbed him greatly.)*

10. What did Perry do immediately after the murders? What did Dick do, and why did his father find this strange? What do these actions reveal about Dick and Perry? *(Perry fell asleep in a hotel room after taking off his boots and leaving them to soak in a washbasin. Dick returned home, ate dinner with his family, and fell asleep watching television. His family was "not conscious of anything uncommon in his manner" [p. 73] until the Hickock men went into the living room to watch a televised basketball game and Dick fell asleep shortly after it began. Dick's father stated that "he never thought he'd live to see the day when Dick would rather sleep than watch basketball" [pp. 73–74]. Answers will vary, but most students will note how the two men's seemingly calm, normal activities reveal their lack of thought and regret for their crime. That they can simply fall asleep after having brutally murdered four people is evidence of their cruel natures [and possibly, their abnormal mental states].)*

### Supplementary Activities

1. Complete a Word Map (see page 30 of this guide) for at least six vocabulary words from this section.

2. Create a collage or other artistic interpretation of Dick and Perry at the gas station, their last stop before the murders. Use symbols and images to depict how each feels about their plan, about themselves, and about each other.

## Part II: Persons Unknown
## Pages 75–117

Capote details how the community of Holcomb went about burying the Clutter family and cleaning their home. The Kansas Bureau of Investigation (KBI) assigned the case to Alvin Adams Dewey of Garden City, Kansas. A total of 18 men were eventually assigned to the case full time, and Dewey's personal team—including Agents Nye, Church, and Duntz—played key roles in tracking down Dick and Perry, a difficult task considering the utter lack of evidence. They scoured the frightened community for any clues and chased down numerous rumors and wild theories concerning the Clutters' possible enemies. Meanwhile, Perry became obsessed with following the case in the newspapers, terrified that the police would find them. Dick was unconcerned and didn't wish to discuss the case. Dick and Perry decided to secure money to leave town by writing bad checks for cash and merchandise that they sold or stockpiled to sell later. They stole a large amount of money and soon left for Mexico, but their troubles followed them. Perry continued to harp on the murders, and the two men grew weary and suspicious of each other.

### Vocabulary

raucous
tantalized
abstainer
eccentric
abortive
premonition
ardently
speculations
gratify
bereaved
peculiarities
transient
prolific

### Discussion Questions

1. What did Alfred Stoecklein hope people would "try to understand" (p. 78)? Why was he so distraught and confused? *(Mr. Stoecklein was worried that people would speculate about his possible connection to the murders, specifically that he lived less than 100 yards from the Clutter home and should have been able to hear the gunshots. He claimed the wind was blowing in the wrong direction and a large barn stands between the two houses. He hoped people understood that he couldn't have possibly heard anything and that he had nothing to do with the crime. Answers will vary, but students should consider that Alfred Stoecklein knew how quickly rumors could spread in Holcomb and he was worried for his family's reputation. He was also frightened because of the murders and decided to move to a house along the highway, where he and his wife would feel safer.)*
2. What was the first thing Agent Alvin Dewey told the press, and what facts did he make known? *(The first thing Dewey told the journalists is that he would "talk facts but not theories" [p. 81] when it came to the Clutter case. He stressed the fact that they were dealing with four murders, not just one, and they didn't know if one or all four victims were the main target of the murderers. Investigators suspected Herb Clutter was the main target since he was cut, shot, and tortured. Investigators had not yet discovered a motive and didn't yet know in what order the Clutters were killed. As far as they knew, nothing had been stolen and neither Mrs. Clutter nor Nancy had been "sexually molested." Agent Dewey admitted that Herb Clutter buying so much life insurance the day before his death was strange, but he didn't believe it was linked to the crime.)*
3. Explain Agent Dewey's two "concepts" regarding who murdered the Clutter family. Which did he believe was true? *(the "single-killer concept," in which the murderer was believed to be a friend or close acquaintance of the Clutter family, and the "double-killer concept," in which the murderer had an accomplice; Agent Dewey favored the second concept, because he believes Herb and Kenyon would have been able to fight off just one man.)*
4. What possible motives did Agent Dewey discover in Nancy Clutter's diary, and how did he feel about each of these? *(Agent Dewey gleaned two possible motives from Nancy's diary. One included angst from Mr. Clutter telling Nancy to stop seeing Bobby Rupp so often. Although Agent Dewey didn't believe that Bobby had anything to do with the murders, he was "the only person to whom a motive, however feeble, could be attributed" [p. 84]. He also read a passage in the diary about the family cat mysteriously dying, supposedly from poisoning. Agent Dewey thought this might show that someone held a grudge against the Clutters and decided to kill them. Nancy wrote that she buried the cat in a special place, and Agent Dewey hoped to find the cat's grave and test his theory.)*
5. What made the police first believe that robbery was the motive for the murders, and what evidence was there to refute that idea? *(Agent Nye believed the entire setup "ha[d] that robbery smell" [p. 86], mainly because Mr. Clutter's wallet was disturbed and Nancy's purse was lying open on the kitchen floor. Investigators only found $2 in the house, which was strange because Mr. Clutter had cashed a check for $60 just the day before. However, no jewelry was stolen and Herb's aversion to carrying cash was legendary in the area. Investigators felt that the small amount of money in the house wouldn't possibly be worth killing four people.)*

6. Describe Dick's and Perry's attitude in the days following the murders, and how did each react to the stories in the newspapers? *(Perry became paranoid and constantly monitored the newspapers, so much so that he was unable to eat. He was very suspicious that the newspapers reported there were no clues in the case. He didn't believe that was true, but instead that the police and newspapers must be trying to trap them. Dick was bored by the speculation and ignored the newspaper stories. He was completely unconcerned with Perry's worries, saying "We scored. It was perfect" [p. 90]. Dick didn't want to think about the murders ever again.)*
7. According to Susan, how did Bobby react to the news and investigation of the murders? How did the murders affect Susan and Bobby's friendship? *(The ordeal affected Bobby greatly because he had never suffered through any tragedies before. Bobby not only had to deal with the death of his girlfriend but also with a lie-detector test and early accusations that he was the killer, although he wasn't "bitter about that; he realized the police were doing what they had to do" [p. 94]. Susan and Bobby began to spend more time together. Bobby would often say that he would never love another girl, but Susan assured him that Nancy would not have wanted him to think that way.)*
8. Describe Dick's plan for raising enough money to get out of town. What role does Perry play in this scheme? *(Dick and Perry traveled to several stores, telling the clerks that Perry was getting married and they needed clothing and gifts. Dick conveniently "forgot" his wallet each time, so they wrote fake checks for more than the amount of their purchases, and received the difference in cash. Perry was supposed to just go along and smile, leaving all of the talking to Dick. The plan worked, and the two men raised enough money to escape Kansas.)*
9. Why did Dick feel so bad about his fake check scheme, and how did Perry try to assuage Dick's guilt? *(Dick felt guilty about scamming the stores because his parents would have to deal with the problem when the stores could not locate Dick. His father is old and sick, and this weighed on Dick's mind. Perry tried to tell him that the two of them could pay off the debt from Mexico once they started making money.)*
10. What about the murder scene weighed on Agent Dewey's mind and made him speculate about the mindset of the murderers? *(Agent Dewey was intrigued by the fact that the murderers placed the mattress box underneath Herb Clutter before they killed him. He also noticed that whoever tied up Nancy and Mrs. Clutter pulled the blankets up around their bodies, as if tucking them into bed, and a pillow had been placed under Kenyon's head. Agent Dewey wondered at such special care taken by the murderers to make the Clutters comfortable. These oddities seemed to hint that the murderers had some sympathy for their victims.)*
11. How did Perry feel after the murders, and how did Dick respond? *(Perry had doubts about everything. He pondered, "I think there must be something wrong with us. To do what we did" [p. 108], "...I never thought I could do it. A thing like that" [p. 109], and "...I don't see how it's possible. To do what we did. And just one hundred percent get away with it" [p. 109]. Dick was unconcerned and content, certain that Perry was being paranoid. However, the more Perry spoke his doubts aloud, the more Dick worried that Perry might be right. He snapped at Perry to "...just shut up" [p. 110].)*

## Supplementary Activities

1. Research the symbols and animals in Perry's dreams (pages 92–93 of the book), and create a collage or poster that includes information about what each could mean. You may also include the importance these elements have from a psychological or cultural standpoint.
2. Write a one-page letter to the editor from the point of view of one of the residents of Holcomb, explaining your views on the case and how it has negatively affected your life.



 

## Pages 117–155

Perry and Dick enjoyed life in Mexico, but they soon ran out of money and decided that they could make a better living back in the United States. Perry lamented the fact that he would have to leave behind some of his belongings. While sorting through old letters and journals, Capote and Perry discuss Perry's background and his difficult, poverty-stricken childhood. The letters describe the love-hate relationship Perry has with his sister and father and depict Perry as a troubled wanderer with few friends or realistic aspirations. Back in Kansas, Agent Dewey and his men found few leads in the case, and the townspeople, already terrified that a murderer might be living among them, began to accuse Dewey of not doing enough to solve the case. Dewey visits the abandoned Clutter farm often, contemplating the case and the family.

### Vocabulary

bewitched
prowling
purloined
desperado
aversion
incarnate
effeminate
vagrancy
garnered
conventionalism
paradox
profundity
prognosis
acquiesced
pugnacity
sumptuous

### Discussion Questions

1. What did Paul Helm tell Agent Dewey, and why didn't Dewey believe him? *(Helm claimed he saw two men arrive at the Clutter farm, speak briefly to Herb, and walk away "looking sulky." Agent Dewey seemed to believe Paul was lying in order to mislead the investigators, and chose to believe the insurance agent, Bob Johnson instead—who insisted he was the only visitor to the farm that day.)*
2. Why did Dick grow to despise Mexico, and why did he want to return to the United States? How did Perry feel about this, and what did he finally decide to do? *(With no money left, Dick tried to find a job but was furious that the wage for a mechanic was only two dollars a day, which he finds offensively low. Dick scoffed at the idea of working for such little money when he could make much more doing the same thing in America, so he promptly suggested they leave Mexico as soon as possible. Perry did not like this idea and considered staying in Mexico alone. He was used to the lifestyle of a loner, but he finally gave in to a "newly grown superstitious certainty" [p. 124] about their inevitable capture unless he and Dick stayed together, so he agreed to go back to the United States with Dick.)*
3. Based on his letter, do you think Perry's father knows Perry's true nature? Why or why not? *(Answers will vary. There are many aspects of the letter that may not align with what we know about Perry. Some examples include his father's repeated assurance that Perry will never find himself in trouble with the law again and has "learned a lesson he will never forget" [p. 129]. He says Perry knows that the "*law is boss*" and that he "wont [sic] steal a cent from a friend or anyone else" [p. 130]. He claims that his son avoids bad people and enjoys being with "outdoors people," which doesn't seem to be the case. It is evident that the two have spent a lot of time together but Perry's father doesn't know him as well as he thinks. Perry may have acted differently around his father and told him things he wanted to hear, or his father just may not wish to believe anything bad about his son. Perry's father is obviously attempting to sway those in authority to believe that his son is worthy of a decent life outside of prison.)*
4. To what does Perry attribute his bed-wetting, and why does he despise nuns? *(When his parents were traveling and living out of the back of a truck, they had little to eat. One of their dietary staples was "Hawks Brand condensed milk," the sugar content of which "weakened [his] kidneys" [p. 131]. Perry believes this is what started his cycle of bed-wetting, and his time spent living with nuns only made it worse because they would hit him when it happened. Their cruel treatment left Perry with a lifelong aversion to nuns in particular and religion in general.)*

5. How did Perry and his father waste their time and money, and how did Perry's father react to the situation? *(After Perry left the military and recovered from his motorcycle accident, he helped his father build a large hunting lodge and roadside motel in rural Alaska. The arduous project took a great deal of time to complete and sapped them of all their strength and money, but the prospective hunters and travelers never materialized and the project ended in failure. Perry's father, distraught over this failure, blamed his son for their misfortune. Perry said his father would "Boss [him] around. Be spiteful. Say [he] didn't do [his] proper share of the work" [p. 135]. Perry's father eventually threw him out of the lodge. Perry picked up his guitar, left everything else on the ground where his father dumped it, and left for good.)*

6. What might Perry's sister mean when she writes to him, "IT IS NO SHAME TO HAVE A DIRTY FACE—THE SHAME COMES WHEN YOU <u>KEEP</u> IT DIRTY" (p. 140)? *(Answers will vary. Suggestions: She may be trying to tell her brother that bad things have happened to them in the past and that everyone has personal blemishes and unappealing traits but they need to work on overcoming them. This is backhanded advice because she is accusing Perry of not recognizing his problems or trying to fix them. She believes that Perry needs to take responsibility for his own life because their father is not responsible for Perry's misdeeds. She feels that Perry has never considered others' feelings and the shame is his for not trying to amend his life.)*

7. How does Perry truly feel about his sister and her letter? Why does he keep it? *(Perry loathes his sister and claims he wishes she had been in the Clutter house when he and Dick arrived, implying that he wants her dead. Perry keeps the letter because Willie-Jay read and wrote an analysis of the letter for Perry, and it is this response from Willie-Jay that Perry truly values.)*

8. What did Willie-Jay say about the letter from Perry's sister? Do you agree with each of his statements? Why or why not? *(Willie-Jay said that Perry's sister claims to demonstrate Christian principles but her letter is judgmental and reveals a hidden temper. He advised Perry not to write back, claiming that "It is a foolish letter, but born of human failing" [p. 143]. He also stated that Perry's sister cannot fathom the pressures that Perry must deal with and that she never will. Willie-Jay believes that Perry's sister is jealous that her father has always favored Perry, and he also thinks Perry's father has taken advantage of this, painting himself to be a victim in his daughter's eyes and thus earning more of her respect. Willie-Jay insisted that she is not sorry [as she says she is] that the letter must go through a censor; instead, she added this as a subtle reminder to the authorities that the Smith family are not all bad and not to judge them based on Perry's actions. Finally, Willie-Jay told Perry that letters to his sister "cannot serve anything but a purely social function" [p. 145] and not to put too much of his emotional energy into writing her, should he choose to do so again. Answers will vary.)*

9. How do the Clutter murders continue to affect Agent Dewey's life? *(The case is dominating his life; he is "haunted" by the Clutters. It is all he talks and thinks about, with the hope that by talking about it he might stumble upon new clues or new angles. He is afraid that if he does not solve the case soon, he will obsess over it the rest of his life, always connecting future cases with this one. Also, certain townspeople are blaming him for the case remaining unsolved.)*

### Supplementary Activities

1. Examine the words that Perry thought were "beautiful" or "useful" on page 146 of the book. Choose three of these words, and explain in a few sentences why you think Perry would find them important.

2. Complete the Thought Bubble activity on page 31 of this guide, expressing Perry's thoughts when he read his sister's letter for the first time.



 

## Part III: Answer Pages 157–198

Floyd Wells, a convict who was once Dick's cellmate, heard of the murders and recalled working for the Clutter family. He claimed that he told Dick that Mr. Clutter was a wealthy man who had a safe in his office, to which Dick replied that he planned to go there someday and kill the family in order to steal the money. After great deliberation, Wells came forward with this information and the police now had their first real suspects. Agent Nye began to interview those who know Dick and Perry, gathering evidence for a case against the two men. Meanwhile, Dick and Perry traveled across the United States, trying to lay low. After once again running out of money, they decided to return to Kansas City, much to Perry's chagrin.

| Vocabulary |
|---|
| ruination<br>ascertained<br>corroborated<br>subdued<br>conceited<br>palliatives<br>ambivalent<br>fortitude<br>pathological<br>commodity<br>permeated<br>urchin<br>cavalcade<br>trivialities<br>delirium<br>invulnerable |

### Discussion Questions

1. Who is Floyd Wells, and what did he tell Dick? Why did he take so long to speak to the police after hearing about the Clutter murders? Do you think the police should believe Floyd's story? Why or why not? *(He is a prisoner in Kansas State Penitentiary and Dick's former cellmate. Floyd used to work at the Clutter farm, and he told Dick that Mr. Clutter was a wealthy man who had a safe in his office. He was afraid to speak to the police because if other prisoners heard him talking to the police, they would kill him. He was also wary that by telling Dick about the Clutters, and thereby giving him a motive for the crime, he [Floyd] might be implicated in their murders. Answers will vary. Discussion should cover the merit of a convicted felon's word and whether or not Floyd Wells had anything to gain by lying about Dick.)*
2. What did Dick's parents tell Agent Nye regarding all of their son's troubles? What do they think of Perry? *(Dick's mother defended her son, unable to understand why he always gets into trouble [although she blames Perry for some of it]. Dick's father used to be very proud of his son but said that after [Dick's] car accident "he wasn't the same boy" [p. 166] and that going to prison the first time caused him to become "a plain stranger" [p. 167]. Neither parent believes Dick is capable of murder. When Dick brought Perry to visit, his parents "wouldn't have [Perry] in the house" [p. 169]. The Hickocks made it very clear to Agent Nye that they didn't like Perry's appearance or his background and they're sure he is the one who got Dick into so much trouble.)*
3. What did Dick and Perry plan to do once they found a ride to Nebraska, and why was Perry bothered by this plan? How was their plan foiled? *(Once Dick and Perry found a ride, they planned to kill the driver and steal the car. Dick would sit next to the driver and distract him. Dick would cue Perry with, "Hey, Perry, pass me a match" [p. 173] and then grab the steering wheel as Perry bludgeoned the driver from behind. Once in the car, Dick kept talking to the driver, and Perry grew impatient and annoyed, almost disgusted by how Dick attempted to "impress a man [he was] going to kill" [p. 173]. This bothered him more than the idea of killing a man for his car. Just as Dick cued Perry, the driver pulled over to pick up a third hitchhiker.)*
4. What did the landlady tell Agent Nye about Perry, and what did Nye find in Perry's box? *(She confirmed that Perry stayed in her Las Vegas rooming house a few times and left most recently just prior to the Clutter murders. She said Perry was "only a punk" [p. 176] who tried to sweet-talk her out of having to pay rent. Perry had no friends, worked on a car in the parking lot, and sold it for*

*money to buy a bus ticket, although she doesn't know where to. She showed Agent Nye a cardboard box full of personal belongings Perry left behind. In the box, Nye found towels and pillows from the motel, old clothing, souvenirs from various cities, a scrapbook "thick with photographs" [p. 178] from weight-lifting magazines, and a collection of medicines [particularly an excessive amount of aspirin].)*

5. According to her discussion with Agent Nye, how does Perry's sister feel about him, and why did she write him so often when he was in prison? What is important about the fact that Perry's sister never lived in Fort Scott, Kansas? *(She says that she is afraid of Perry and asks Agent Nye to keep her current address from him. She insists that Perry "has no respect for anyone" [p. 181] and isn't surprised that he is in trouble again. She claims to have written him so often because she once had hopes that she "might change a few of his ideas" [p. 181]. The fact that Perry's sister never lived in Kansas proves that Dick and Perry lied about their alibi and could likely have committed the Clutter murders.)*

6. How does Perry feel about all of his siblings? What eventually happened to them? *(In an argument with his sister, Perry revealed that he hates all of his siblings and thinks they were treated better because they each got an education. He was drunk during this argument, and he pushed his sister against a wall, yelling about not liking himself and never getting the chance to go to school like his siblings. He threatened to kill her if she didn't listen to him, and he concluded that he hated her as well as his father. Perry's brother Jimmy killed himself, and his sister Fern changed her name to Joy and became an alcoholic. She later allegedly fell out of a hotel window and died. While Perry fell into a life of crime, Barbara is the only sibling who found some sort of normalcy.)*

7. What was Dick's ultimate plan, and how did Perry feel about it? What was Perry's biggest concern? *(The two men did not have any money, and Dick was certain that he could write more bad checks in Kansas City. Perry argued that returning to Kansas was "a crazy-man stunt" [p. 188] because Dick was surely wanted for parole violation by that time. Perry also did not want to return to the state in which they had committed murder. Dick scoffed at Perry and asked why he couldn't just forget the murders. He said, "They never made any connection. They never will" [p. 188]. Perry continued to protest, saying that if Dick was wrong about the police not looking for them, they would both end up in "The Corner," inmates' name for Death Row in Kansas.)*

8. Why didn't Agent Dewey wish to reveal his suspects to the media or to the public? *(He wanted to be very careful about how he proceeded since "[there was] a possibility these men [were] innocent" [p. 189]. Since a criminal was their only informant, Dewey wanted to verify every lead and amass as much evidence as possible. He also didn't want to alert Dick and Perry that the police were looking for them. Dewey wanted them to let down their guard in the hopes that they slipped up. Still, he hoped to capture them as soon as possible because "the longer they're free, the less of a case [the investigators would] have" [pp. 189–190].)*

9. Why is news about the Clutter case spreading faster in Garden City than in Holcomb? *(Holcomb residents are exasperated with the topic and refuse to go on being distrustful and scared. Garden City residents are still fascinated with the crime and continue to speculate on the identity of the murderer[s].)*

10. What did Perry worry about while he waited for Dick at the washateria? Describe Perry's level of trust in Dick. *(Perry feared that Dick had been arrested for the bad checks or their stolen car and was presently "spill[ing] his guts" [p. 193] to the police about the Clutter murders. Perry becomes sick with worry while waiting for Dick to return. He is extremely worried about being back in Kansas City, and his paranoia that the police are onto them makes him wonder about Dick's resolve to stay true to their partnership. He realizes how petty Dick is, how he is "an urchin*



 

*dependent...on stolen coins" [p. 193]. Perry continues to vacillate about Dick's resolve and dedication to their partnership until Dick eventually arrives. Perry's trust in Dick is shaky at best, and the very things that bind them—the murders, for instance—are the same things that are creating paranoia and distrust. While Perry despises Dick, he also needs him.)*

### Supplementary Activities

1. In a brief essay, explain why Perry and his sister are jealous of each other, specifically in regard to their father. Why is this jealousy misplaced and/or ironic?
2. Describe Perry using the Character Analysis Blocks on page 32 of this guide.

## Pages 199–248

After running another series of successful cons in Kansas City, Dick and Perry went to Florida and spent their days beachside. Their distrust of one another increases, and Perry grows more disgusted with Dick's casual, lewd behavior. They decided to keep moving west, eventually all the way back to Las Vegas where Perry hoped to pick up a box of his personal belongings. The police are waiting for them in Las Vegas, and the two are finally arrested. They are interrogated separately, and after maintaining a casual, almost haughty demeanor throughout, Dick realizes that he is trapped and confesses, blaming Perry for the murders. Perry, shocked to hear that Dick talked, reveals many details from the night of the murder, walking the investigators step-by-step through the crime.

| Vocabulary |
|---|
| afflicted |
| reveries |
| somnolent |
| succumbed |
| fervor |
| circumstantial |
| reconnoiter |
| extradition |
| recapitulation |
| allusions |
| sanctuary |
| premeditation |
| festooning |
| fragmentary |
| conjectured |
| expurgated |
| fusillade |
| retribution |

### Discussion Questions

1. What element about Dick's personality bothers Perry, particularly while they hid in Florida? How does Dick feel about this part of his personality? *(Perry despises that Dick is a rapist, as Perry has "no respect for people who can't control themselves sexually" [p. 202], especially those who, like Dick, are often "bothering kids." This sense of morality is honorable yet ironic since Perry is a mass murderer who doesn't think much of anyone but himself. Dick "was sorry he felt as he did" [p. 201] about young girls, but he still believes that his feelings are normal.)*
2. How did Perry and Dick initially feel about the hitchhikers? How did the hitchhikers prove their "value" along the way? *(Perry wanted to pick them up right away, but Dick was unsure because the hitchhikers did not look "as if they could pay their way" [p. 207]. Once Dick realized that the old man was sick, he wanted to get rid of the hitchhikers, telling Perry to "use [his] head. Just for once...Suppose he dies" [p. 209]? Perry stood up for the hitchhikers and assured Dick that if he kicked them out, he would get out, too. The hitchhikers told Dick and Perry that if they drove slower, they could find empty bottles along the roadside that could be turned in for money.)*

3. What concerns does Agent Dewey have even after apprehending Dick and Perry? *(Even though Dick and Perry are now in custody, Agent Dewey is still worried that he doesn't have enough evidence to prove they were in the Clutter house and certainly not enough to convict them. Because he has so little hard evidence, Dewey knows that "if they didn't confess they could never be convicted" [p. 213]. At the moment, Dick and Perry believe they were arrested for parole violations and writing bad checks. They have no idea that the police suspect them of the Clutter murders. Dewey wants to "hit" them with this information so that they confess.)*
4. What was Dick's plan in Las Vegas, and why didn't it work? *(Dick planned to impersonate an Air Force officer and write more bad checks throughout the city. He hoped to "crawl the strip" and acquire "three, maybe four thousand dollars within a twenty-four-hour period" [p. 214]. After this, he planned to leave town without Perry: "[He] was sick of him...he was like a wife that must be got rid of" [pp. 214–215]. This plan never came to fruition because the police spotted their stolen car and arrested them.)*
5. What did the investigators think about Dick when they first met him? How does Dick initially react to his interrogation? *(The Kansas agents imagined a bigger, brawnier man, "not some skinny kid" [p. 216]. They found Dick to be "clean, polite, [with a] nice voice, good diction, a pretty decent-looking fellow, with a very disarming smile" [p. 216]. Dick is incredibly confident and relaxed. He is polite to the agents, and he smiles and jokes a lot during the beginning of the interrogation. He lies easily and seems unconcerned, telling them, "I know the form...I've been questioned before" [p. 217].)*
6. How does Dick react when the agents mention the Clutter family? How do the police finally pressure Dick to confess? *(When Agent Nye mentions the Clutters, Dick has "an intense visible reaction" [p. 223]. He turns gray, and his eyes begin to twitch. He immediately states that he is not a killer, but the agents counter that they merely asked if he knew of the case, not if he killed anyone. They tell Dick that he made two mistakes while committing the crime, one being leaving behind a living witness. Dick's reaction, declaring this impossible, helps incriminate him. Dick finally confesses when shown his own boots and is told there are bloody footprints. He declares that "Perry Smith killed the Clutters...It was Perry. I couldn't stop him. He killed them all" [p. 230].)*
7. How does Perry behave throughout his interrogation? How is he convinced that Dick has confessed? *(Perry is even more relaxed than Dick, although he does not joke with the agents or exhibit much emotion at all. He also lies easily and refuses to be rattled when the Clutters are mentioned. Agent Dewey tells Perry that Dick blamed the four murders entirely on Perry, but Perry doesn't believe him. When Dewey mentions that Dick told the story about Perry killing a man in Las Vegas, Perry realizes that Dick has in fact talked.)*
8. Just as Dick and Perry approached the Clutter house, what happened that almost saved the Clutters' lives? What ultimately convinced Dick to proceed? *(As Dick and Perry sat in the car on the dark road near the Clutter house, they saw a light come on in a house nearby. This gave the men pause. The light continued to flash on and off, making the men think someone was up very late at night. Perry said he told Dick to "count [him] out" [p. 235] and to abandon the plan or to go alone. Dick started the car, to Perry's relief, but halfway down the road Dick stopped again. He was furious about setting up "this big score" [p. 235] and now Perry wanted to "chicken out." Dick said he could do it alone if he had to and turned around again, bringing them back to the Clutters' farm.)*
9. How does Agent Dewey feel after Perry tells the story of how he helped murder the Clutter family? *(He feels sorrow and profound fatigue after hearing Perry's description of the murders. He feels as though the crime lacks purpose or a "meaningful design"; the fact that the Clutters were killed by complete strangers for no reason at all makes it seem even more terrible. Without a rational explanation for* why *the crime was committed, Agent Dewey does not feel any better about solving*



 

*the case. He also feels a certain amount of sympathy for Perry, for although Perry has just described a heinous act which caused terrible suffering for the Clutter family, Agent Dewey pities him for his "ugly and lonely" [p. 246] life. However, he does not believe Perry and Dick deserve mercy.)*

10. What is the only discrepancy in Perry and Dick's stories? Whom do you believe, and why? *(Perry states that each of them killed two people, but Dick claims that Perry killed all four of the Clutters. Answers will vary.)*

### Supplementary Activities

1. Using the newspaper headline on page 247 of the book, "FEAR LYNCH MOB AWAITING RETURN OF KILLER SUSPECTS," write the first three paragraphs of the news story using what you know about Dick and Perry's capture and the charges they are facing. Give your news story to a classmate, and have them write three more paragraphs to finish the story. Read the news story to the class.
2. Research police interrogation and interview techniques, and list three things the police did that were effective in gaining key information from Dick and Perry.

## Part IV: The Corner
## Pages 249–292

Dick and Perry are extradited to Finney County, Kansas, where they are appointed lawyers and await their trial. As the jury selection begins, the Clutter family's belongings are auctioned off and the painful feelings within the community are brought forth, casting a pall on the trial. Dick and Perry receive letters and visits from friends and family. The evidence against the two defendants is substantial, especially the statements they made to the police and the footprints they left behind. The images of the murdered Clutter family horrify the courtroom, though Dick's father constantly rails against the proceedings and the judge, calling the entire ordeal a farce. Capote shares two autobiographical statements Perry and Dick wrote for a psychiatrist, each revealing intimate details about their childhoods, the murders, and each other. Both Perry and Dick dream of escaping. Donald Cullivan, Perry's former Army friend, visits him in jail and tries to convince Perry to show remorse and turn to God, but Perry rejects this suggestion.

### Discussion Questions

1. What is unique about the fourth floor of the courthouse and about Perry's cell in particular? *(The fourth floor is part jailhouse, part apartment, the residence of Wendle and Josephine Meier. Wendle is the undersheriff, and Josephine helps take care of prisoners held in the courthouse. There are six cells on the floor, five for men and one for a woman. Perry's jail cell is normally reserved for female prisoners. It is an isolated cell situated inside the Meiers' residence with a window through which he can speak to Mrs. Meier. Perry was placed here in order to separate him from Dick.)*

| Vocabulary |
|---|
| mélange<br>monotonous<br>idyllic<br>stiletto<br>periphery<br>cantankerous<br>mirthless<br>unpretentious<br>odious<br>ministrations<br>vicissitudes<br>beleaguered<br>chagrined<br>contrition |

2. What part of his story does Perry eventually change, and why? *(Perry first claimed that Dick killed Bonnie and Nancy Clutter, but he changes his story to include that he [Perry] killed all four members of the Clutter family. Perry says he lied because he wanted to "fix Dick for being such a coward" [p. 255]. But he actually just feels sorry for Dick's mother and doesn't want her to think that her son is a murderer, calling Mrs. Hickock "a real sweet person" [p. 255].)*

3. How do the two court-appointed lawyers feel about defending Perry and Dick? How do you think this will affect the case? *(Perry's lawyer, Arthur Fleming, does not want to accept the appointment, but he knows he has no choice. Dick's lawyer, Harrison Smith, is not very happy about it either, but he knows someone has to do it and vows to do his best. Answers will vary. Some students might feel that by publicly admitting their hesitancy, the lawyers have already done their clients a disservice. By law, Perry and Dick deserve a fair trial, but having disinterested lawyers representing them could lead to a trial that is biased or unfair. Other students may feel that since Perry and Dick already confessed, there is not much further damage their lawyers' feelings could do.)*

4. While Dick and Perry wait for the trial to begin, what does each of them think about in his cell? *(Perry is very lonely in his cell. Aside from befriending a squirrel and occasionally speaking to Mrs. Meier, he wishes he could speak to Dick. Although he despises Dick's cowardice, Perry feels closest to him because they are "of the same species" [p. 260] and he feels extremely alone. Dick isn't so much lonely as bored. His cell is not as isolated as Perry's, and he sometimes has other inmates to joke and make idle chatter with. He reads magazines, chews gum, whistles his favorite songs, and quietly plans to "bust jail. Grab a car and raise dust" [p. 263]. Few of his thoughts are of Perry.)*

5. Who writes to Perry, and what does this person wish to do? *(Don Cullivan, who served with Perry in the Army, hears of Perry's legal troubles and wishes to help him in any way he can. Perry is thrilled, grateful, and excited that "a sane and respectable man" [p. 262] considers Perry a friend and wants to help him.)*

6. Why do Dick and Perry's lawyers want the trial postponed? Do you think their reasons are valid? Why or why not? *(Dick's father, "a most material witness" [p. 268], is too ill to testify, and the Clutter estate auction is to be held the day before the trial starts. The lawyers claim that the advertisements for this auction will be a painful reminder of the crime for the prospective jurors. The judge denies their motion. Answers will vary. Students should discuss the effectiveness of Dick's father as a witness, the bias the prospective jurors may feel because of the auction [or already feel because of the Clutters being beloved in the community], and the chances that Dick and Perry would be found innocent if the trial were delayed.)*

7. In Dick's autobiographical statement, what does he reveal about his true intentions the night of the Clutter murders? How does he feel about this in retrospect, and how were his intentions thwarted? *(While the story he told cellmates and Perry was that he wanted to rob the Clutter farm, in the back of his mind he "knew there would be a girl there" and that he intended "to rape the girl" [p. 278]. He admits that he thought about it a lot and it is why he didn't want to turn back when Perry insisted they should and why he continued even after failing to find the alleged safe. Looking back, Dick knows it was wrong, "but at the time [he] never [gave] any thought to whether it [was] right or wrong" [p. 278] because it is "an impulse" that he cannot control. Dick was unable to carry out his intentions because Perry would not allow it.)*

8. Who is the prosecution's "most damaging witness" (p. 286), and what effect does this witness' testimony have on Dick's parents? *(The witness is Agent Dewey, who reveals the intimate details of the murder told to him by both Dick and Perry during their confessions, many of which shock the courtroom audience. Dick's parents are most affected by Dick's intentions of raping Nancy Clutter and by hearing that Perry tried to protect Dick and his mother by claiming that he killed all four members of the Clutter family. Perry's insistence that Dick "didn't want to die with his mother thinking he had killed" and that he [Perry] had obliged because "the Hickocks were good people" [p. 286] pushes Mrs. Hickock over the edge; she begins to cry inconsolably. She wonders how Dick could have become a criminal, trying to figure out how she went wrong in raising him. She claims "there's lots more to Dick than what [people] hear...in the courtroom" [p. 287], although she knows she "can't make any excuses for what he did" [p. 288]. She pities Perry, feeling that "it was wrong of [her] to hate him" [p. 288].)*

9. Describe Don Cullivan's visit with Perry. Why does he visit, and how does Perry react? *("The opportunity to entertain [Cullivan]...delighted Perry" [p. 289], and he prepared a full menu for the dinner they would share in his cell. Perry made meticulous arrangements, and with Mrs. Meier's help, he decorated the table with linens, napkins, china, and silver. Perry seems eager to talk and keep the conversation genial and casual, but Cullivan hopes to steer the conversation toward more spiritual matters. He is determined to save Perry's soul by bringing him to God. Perry rebuffs Don's attempts but is still glad for his visit. He explains to a disbelieving Don that he doesn't feel any remorse for his crime, only regret that he may have to die for it. He threatens to kill himself in front of Don so he can die with "somebody who cares about [him] a little bit" [p. 292].)*

## Supplementary Activities

1. Write a three-page biographical statement about yourself, including your background, personality, and why you think you became the kind of person you are today.
2. Research how juries are selected in your city and/or state, and write a brief essay about how the selection process works. Include three typical questions citizens are asked during selection to see if they are fit to serve on a jury, as well as three reasons why a court might dismiss someone from serving.

## Pages 292–343

The trial continues, and Dick and Perry find themselves fighting a losing battle. After a quick deliberation, the jury finds them guilty and they are sentenced to death by hanging. While on Death Row, Dick reads law books and convinces the Kansas State Bar Association to review the case. After a long series of independent interviews and a hearing, a new judge deems that Dick and Perry received a fair trial. In an attempt to beat the system, Perry stops eating and is eventually hospitalized but later returns to Death Row. Other murderers join them there, and Capote relays each of their gruesome stories. After several stays of execution, Dick and Perry are hung.

| Vocabulary |
| --- |
| conspicuous<br>predisposed<br>innocuous<br>contention<br>debonair<br>perturbed<br>callous<br>unctuous<br>rococo<br>uncongenial<br>anathema<br>pinioned<br>malodorous<br>progeny<br>prevaricate<br>intoned |

### Discussion Questions

1. What are Dr. W. Mitchell Jones' assessments of Dick and Perry? Why is he unable to testify to this in court? *(Dr. Jones believes that Dick exhibits above-average intelligence and shows no signs of mental confusion. He is logical and in touch with reality. Dick's concussion and unconsciousness after his car accident caused blackouts, amnesia, and headaches, which the doctor believes may be cause for concern. He believes Dick shows signs of "emotional abnormality" and is impulsive, doing things without regard to consequences for himself or others. He has low self-esteem and suffers from "a severe character disorder" [p. 295], unable to develop or maintain meaningful personal relationships. Dr. Jones believes that Perry "shows definite signs of severe mental illness" [p. 296]. His childhood was traumatic, and he grew up without love or any sense of morality. Like Dick, Perry exhibits above-average intelligence. However, he is extremely paranoid—he is suspicious, distrustful, and feels he is unfairly treated by others. He wishes for friendship but refuses to confide in anyone, expecting only to be misunderstood or betrayed. The doctor believes that Perry has "an ever-present, poorly controlled rage" [p. 297] that is directed at others as well as himself. He is out of touch with reality and is most certainly a "paranoid schizophrenic" [p. 298]. Because of the M'Naghten Rule, "which contends that if the accused knew the nature of his act, and knew it was wrong, then he is mentally competent and responsible for his actions" [p. 267] and leaves little room for explanation, Dr. Jones is only able to respond with a "yes" or "no" answer.)*

2. Analyze Perry's statement: "I thought [Mr. Clutter] was a very nice gentleman...I thought so right up to the moment I cut his throat...[The Clutters] never hurt me. Like other people. Like people have all my life. Maybe it's just that the Clutters were the ones who had to pay for it" (p. 302). *(Answers will vary, but students will probably note that Perry feels as though no one has ever given him a chance in his life. He feels unloved and is therefore unable to show compassion or love to anyone else. He cannot separate harming an innocent person from the harm he has suffered his entire life, although he is able to recognize that not everyone he hurts has wronged him. The fact that he thought Mr. Clutter was a decent man didn't change the fact that Perry was willing to kill him if the need arose. He acts on impulse, with no thought about the consequences. He is indifferent to others because he was never loved by anyone, particularly his parents.)*

3. What do you think most influenced the jury's verdict? What is the verdict, and how do Perry and Dick react? *(Answers will vary. Logan Green criticizes Dick and Perry's lawyers' abilities to defend them properly. He references scripture relating to murder and its suitable punishment and cites the jury's duty in enforcing the law. He emphasizes the senselessness of the Clutters having to die for $40 and appeals to the jury's sense of honor and bravery, imploring them to sentence Dick and Perry to death. He taunts the jury, daring them to send Dick and Perry back to prison and then ever feel safe in their own homes again. Students should also consider the recent auction of the Clutters' property and the venue of the trial as possible influential factors. The jury's deliberations last 40 minutes, and some people expect the decision to be so short that they never leave their seats in the courtroom. The judge actually leaves the building and has to rush back from his farm to read the verdict, which pronounces Dick and Perry guilty of four counts of murder each. They are sentenced to death. As Dick and Perry leave the courtroom, they joke about how the jurors were certainly not "chicken-hearted." This lasting image appeared in the next morning's newspaper, likely shocking and angering the local readers.)*
4. Who is Lowell Lee Andrews? Why is he on Death Row, and how do Dick and Perry feel about him? *(He is a mild-mannered and intelligent young man with "a second, unsuspected personality, one with stunted emotions and a distorted mind" [p. 312]. Referred to by one newspaper as "The Nicest Boy in Wolcott" [p. 312], Andrews was a college student when he started daydreaming about murdering his family. He killed his entire family, shooting his sister once, his mother six times, and his father 17 times. Andrews lied about the circumstances surrounding his discovery of their bodies, but he eventually confessed to the murders. Andrews stated that he "didn't feel anything about it. The time came, and [he] was doing what [he] had to do. That's all there was to it" [p. 313]. Andrews pleaded innocent by reason of insanity, and doctors concluded that he suffered from "schizophrenia, simple type" [p. 315], but he was still found guilty and sentenced to death. Dick gets along with Andy [as he is called by the other inmates] just fine, but Perry cannot stand him.)*
5. Why do you suppose Perry feels the way he does about Lowell Lee Andrews? *(Answers will vary, but students should note that Perry believes himself to be fairly intelligent. Especially in the company of Dick, whom Perry believes to have numerous personality disorders and loathsome traits, Perry feels superior. When Perry encounters Andrews, who is college-educated and well-read, Perry feels belittled and overshadowed. Andrews compounds these feelings when he constantly corrects Perry's grammar and pronunciation in front of the other inmates. Perry is perhaps both jealous of Andrews and annoyed that Dick finds him so fascinating.)*
6. Describe Perry and Dick's experiences on Death Row. *(Perry sleeps most of the time. Dick reads numerous books and writes letters to his family. He also writes letters to numerous organizations, protesting his conviction and calling the trial "a travesty of due process" [p. 322] because of his and Perry's lawyers' "incompetence and inadequacy" [p. 326], Garden City's "hostile atmosphere," the biased jury, and their denied motion for a change of venue. He pleads for these organizations to assist him in getting a new trial. Both men are miserable—from the noise, the heat, and the stench. They have no radio, no card games, no exercise period, and are not allowed out of their cells except for a shower once a week.)*
7. Who are George York and James Latham, and why are they on Death Row? Examine the significance of Dick's statement upon the boys' arrival: "Yessir...[the death penalty is] very popular in Kansas. Juries hand it out like they were giving candy to kids" (p. 322). *(York and Latham are young Army soldiers who participated in a "cross-country murder spree" [p. 322], claiming seven lives. Their trial attracted nationwide attention, especially from "hordes of teen-aged girls" [p. 322] who found them attractive and personable. York and Latham both believed that "it's a rotten world...There's no answer to it but meanness" [p. 323]. Answers will vary. Students should*

*note that Dick feels as though he and Perry didn't receive a fair trial. He believes the state of Kansas is too quick to sentence men to death. Even before hearing of York and Latham's crimes, he assumes they were wrongfully and hastily sent to Death Row. Furthermore, Dick maintains his innocence in the Clutter murders, saying "There are four killers up here and one railroaded man. I'm no...killer. I never touched a hair on a human head" [p. 325].)*

8. How does Dick feel about capital punishment? Why do you think he feels this way? *(Dick supports capital punishment, so long as he isn't the one dying. He states, "Revenge is all it is, but what's wrong with revenge? It's very important" [p. 335] and "I believe in hanging. Just so long as I'm not the one being hanged" [p. 336]. He goes on to say that if he were related to the Clutters or anyone that George York and James Latham killed, he wouldn't rest until the murderers had been killed. Answers will vary. Dick understands the urge to kill, not only for revenge but for "fun," such as when he ran over the stray dog. Students should discuss Dick's feelings based on his status as a convicted murderer as well as the possibility that he could in fact be innocent of the Clutter murders.)*

9. How does Agent Dewey feel about Dick and Perry's deaths? Why do you suppose he feels the way he does about Perry? *(Agent Dewey is hardly affected by Dick's death, but he feels a small measure of sadness at the death of Perry, someone Dewey always considered a "dwarfish boy-man," "an exiled animal," "a creature walking wounded" [p. 341]. Answers will vary, but students should note that Dick had charisma and was immediately personable, while Perry was perceived as quiet and somewhat withdrawn. Agent Dewey, and in fact most of the people who met Perry, always pitied him to some degree. Perry's childhood, small stature, agreeable demeanor, and matter-of-fact response to his circumstances made Agent Dewey develop a twisted sort of affection for the man.)*

## Supplementary Activities

1. Review Lowell Lee Andrews' farewell message on page 332 of the book. Write one to two paragraphs explaining what you think this message means.
2. Form writing pairs. One person should write an essay explaining why Dick and Perry received a fair trial, and the other person should write a rebuttal supporting the opposite claim. Be sure to include facts and examples from the book, and be prepared to share your point/counterpoint essays with the class.



 

## Post-reading Discussion Questions

1. What role does religion play in the book? *(Answers will vary, but some students may respond that religion's role in the book is closely aligned to defining whether or not a person is a good or decent individual. For example, Don Cullivan is a devout Christian who defies logic by leaving his job and family behind [temporarily] to help Perry. This is a bold and inherently good act motivated by a desire to provide Perry with a chance to experience Heaven. The Clutters were also religious, particularly Mrs. Clutter, and are portrayed as a wholesome, loving family. Willie-Jay is another example of someone who values religion and tries to comfort and aid those in need. Perry, on the other hand, rejected religion and those who tried to force it on him [e.g., Cullivan and Willie-Jay, to a degree]. He said about religion, "That stuff don't ring with me" [p. 291]. Perry's rejection of religion helped to define him as someone who depended only on himself for answers and solace and portrayed him as a lost soul without any guidance. Other students may note that just because someone is religious does not mean they are a good person. For example, the nuns who beat and berated Perry when he was a child prove that religion does not always equate goodness. These nuns and their treatment of him were the primary reason Perry rebuffed all religion and the sincere attempts of those around him to bring him to God. Religion was present during Dick and Perry's trial when both the defense and the prosecution use biblical quotes to sway the jury. In this instance, religion, being so widespread in the community, was being used to manipulate believers.)*

2. Why do you think Truman Capote skipped over the murders in the first section of the book and presented the gruesome facts later? *(Answers will vary. Capote probably skipped over that period of time in order to build suspense. By avoiding describing exactly what happened during the night of the murders, Capote avoids the main subject of the book and keeps readers wondering just what happened. This method also appeals to the morbid sense of human nature, with the grisly details becoming an important feature of the story. By telling what happened during the confessions and the trial, Capote also shows that the story varies depending on who is telling it. Capote uses the murderers' words to tell a tale that he wouldn't have been able to tell otherwise.)*

3. How was Truman Capote able to share so many intimate details about the Clutters and the lives of Dick and Perry? Do you believe Capote was successful in presenting an accurate retelling? *(Capote interviewed dozens of people [some who never even made it into the book] during the entire period of the trial and afterward. He took details from official records and developed a close relationship with the murderers during his many visits and interviews. Armed with this information and research material, Capote was able to reconstruct the lives of the Clutters, the hunt for the killers, and the trial. He was also present for much of the trial and aftermath. Though he may not have had access to records or to clear memories of those he interviewed, he likely reconstructed through creative intuition. This is where the creative writing aspect in "New Journalism" comes into play, where writers take liberties and create dialogue and actions that the writer has no proof ever existed.)*

4. Do you think Perry Smith was a sympathetic character? Why or why not? *(Answers will vary. Some students will say that Perry was not a sympathetic character because he murdered four innocent people and spoke of it so casually. The murders were planned, and Perry had plenty of opportunities to leave, but he didn't. This alone would make him unsympathetic, but Perry also displayed a nasty temper during his time in the Army, where he threw a man off a bridge and bragged about killing other innocent people. He also threatened his sister and said he wished she had been in the Clutter house when he killed the family. Even the doctors during the trial described him as paranoid with rage issues. Some students, however, may point out the fact that Perry had a troubled and essentially loveless childhood where he was mocked and abused by nuns and caretakers, that he stopped Dick from raping Nancy and found that sort of perversion disgusting, and that Perry was an intelligent dreamer who, with more friends and support as a child, may have grown up to be a stable person.)*

5. Do you think Dick Hickock was a sympathetic character? Why or why not? *(Answers will vary. Fewer students are likely to find Dick to be a sympathetic character because his childhood was not as bad as Perry's and he showed less sympathy for the Clutters. While he may not have actually killed the Clutters, he planned the murders and refused to turn around when Perry was eager to leave. His intention was to rape Nancy Clutter, and had Perry not been there, he would have. Capote hinted that Dick had raped before, or at least had had inappropriate contact with female children, and Dick admitted to such compulsions. Dick was also cruel to animals and was a habitual liar and thief.)*

6. Do you think Truman Capote presented a balanced and fair approach to the story of the Clutter murder and the subsequent trial? *(Answers will vary. For the most part, Capote used actual case files and interviews with those involved to form the basis of the book. Some may feel that the Clutter family was described as a little too perfect, thus making their murders seem more tragic; however, Capote did present information that showed the Clutters had just as many problems as the average American middle-class family. Capote also showed all sides of Dick and Perry—their murderous rage, insidious planning, and escape, along with more tender moments, such as Dick's concern for his parents' well-being and Perry's friendship with and respect for Willie-Jay. In almost all cases, Capote showed as many elements of those involved as he could, proving them to be human and complex.)*

7. In what ways were Perry and Dick different, and how were they similar? *(Answers will vary. Perry was introverted and nervous, while Dick was boastful and extroverted. Perry was a worrier by nature, was paranoid of those in power, and seemed to have a hard time making friends, while Dick was a braggart and acted confidently around those he didn't know, easily making small talk with almost anyone. Perry was a dreamer and was creative, showing an interest in music, poetry, and books, while Dick was a bit more pragmatic and was a planner. Dick had trouble controlling his sexual urges and tried to take advantage of young girls while Perry found this behavior disgusting. Students should be able to find many other differences between the two men. Similarities include that both Perry and Dick were compelled to murder for reasons besides just money—Perry out of some sense of revenge and belief that Dick would stop him and Dick just because he wanted to. Both men despised authority. Neither man wept or begged for forgiveness [as some thought they might] when they were hung, although Perry did apologize for his actions to those in attendance.)*

8. What was the most uplifting moment in the book? the most frightening? *(Answers will vary. Examples of uplifting moments: Agent Dewey's relief when he apprehended Dick and Perry, Dewey's discussion with Susan Kidwell at the end of the book, Herb Clutter helping members of his community, and possibly even the moment when Perry made friends with a squirrel while in the county jail; Examples of frightening moments: when Bobby Rupp left the Clutter home for the last time and sensed that someone else was there, Susan Kidwell and Nancy Ewalt discovering Nancy Clutter's body, the scenes depicting the Clutter murders as told by Dick and Perry, and Dick and Perry's executions)*

9. Do you think this book is still relevant in modern society? Why or why not? *(Answers will vary. The book is one of the first to give a detailed account of a mass murder, the hunt for the killers, and the trial. This type of story, both fictional and real, has become a huge part of mainstream literature and is always a major story in the news, capturing the attention of thousands, sometimes millions of people. Because of the location of the murder—a rural, small town stereotypical of middle America—and those who were killed—a classic American family—the story is more shocking and catches people off guard because it is so unexpected. These same reactions are seen after crimes that take place in recent years as well—the belief that "it could never happen here" and the shock when it does. The book showed America that murder can reach into any community, no matter how remote and simple, and this threat persists today. For this and other reasons, this book is still relevant.)*

## Post-reading Extension Activities

### Writing

1. Write a ten-line poem about someone from *In Cold Blood* (besides Dick and Perry), omitting the name. Exchange poems with a classmate, and attempt to guess the identity of the person in the poem. For examples of poetic styles, ask your librarian or teacher for books of poetry to read and review.
2. Write a one-page letter (at least three paragraphs) to Agent Dewey as he is investigating the Clutter murders. Include any advice, warnings, or questions you might have for him.

### Reading

3. Read another book written in New Journalism style, and compare this book to *In Cold Blood.*
4. Read a professional book review of *In Cold Blood* (you can find many online), and write a one-page response either agreeing or disagreeing with the critic. Support your opinion with facts from the book.
5. Read one of Truman Capote's other books, and explain at least three similar themes the book shares with *In Cold Blood.*

### Film/Drama

6. Watch one of the film versions of the events in *In Cold Blood,* and write a three-page analysis of the film, comparing and contrasting it to the book. Which do you think tells the story in a more effective way, and why?
7. Cast your own actors for a film version of *In Cold Blood.* Use the character list in this guide as a basis. Choose an actor for each character, and in a paragraph for each, explain how and why your chosen actor exhibits the same traits and ideals as the character.

### Art

8. Examine the cover of *In Cold Blood,* and create a new design that matches a theme from the book. Present your design to the class in a drawing, painting, or photograph (your own or found elsewhere). Be sure the design includes the title and author information, as well as a new tagline or teaser similar to the one currently on the cover.
9. Choose a character from the book, and paint a picture or create a collage with images, symbols, and/or words that represent that character's importance in *In Cold Blood.*
10. For each section of this guide, choose a symbol that represents the major action or tone of that section. Create a poster showing your symbols, and present your artwork in class.

## Assessment for *In Cold Blood*

Assessment is an ongoing process. The following ten items can be completed during study of the book. Once finished, the student and teacher will check the work. Points may be added to indicate the level of understanding.

Name ____________________________________________ Date ____________________

| Student | Teacher | |
|---|---|---|
| ______ | ______ | 1. Write a one-page essay explaining a trait of Agent Alvin Dewey's that you admire and one you do not. |
| ______ | ______ | 2. Complete the Story Map on page 33 of this guide. |
| ______ | ______ | 3. Using 15 vocabulary words from this guide, write a two-page synopsis of *In Cold Blood*. |
| ______ | ______ | 4. Write three review questions about the book, and participate in a class oral review. |
| ______ | ______ | 5. Write a one-page essay about one type of conflict in the book, including whom it involves, how it develops, and how it is resolved. |
| ______ | ______ | 6. Look online for an interview with Truman Capote, and write a one-page essay discussing the interview. |
| ______ | ______ | 7. Write an acrostic poem about a character or a theme from *In Cold Blood* using the title of the book. |
| ______ | ______ | 8. Complete the Cause/Effect Chart on page 34 of this guide. Then, write a paragraph explaining whether you think Floyd Wells is responsible for the Clutters' murders. |
| ______ | ______ | 9. Write a recommendation for *In Cold Blood* explaining what you liked and/or disliked about the book. |
| ______ | ______ | 10. Correct all quizzes taken over the course of reading the book. |



 

## Characterization

**Directions:** Place one of the following character's names in the center circle: Herb Clutter, Nancy Clutter, Dick Hickock, Perry Smith. Brainstorm four of this character's most prominent qualities, and place them in the ovals surrounding the center circle. In the rectangles, list details from the story that demonstrate each quality.

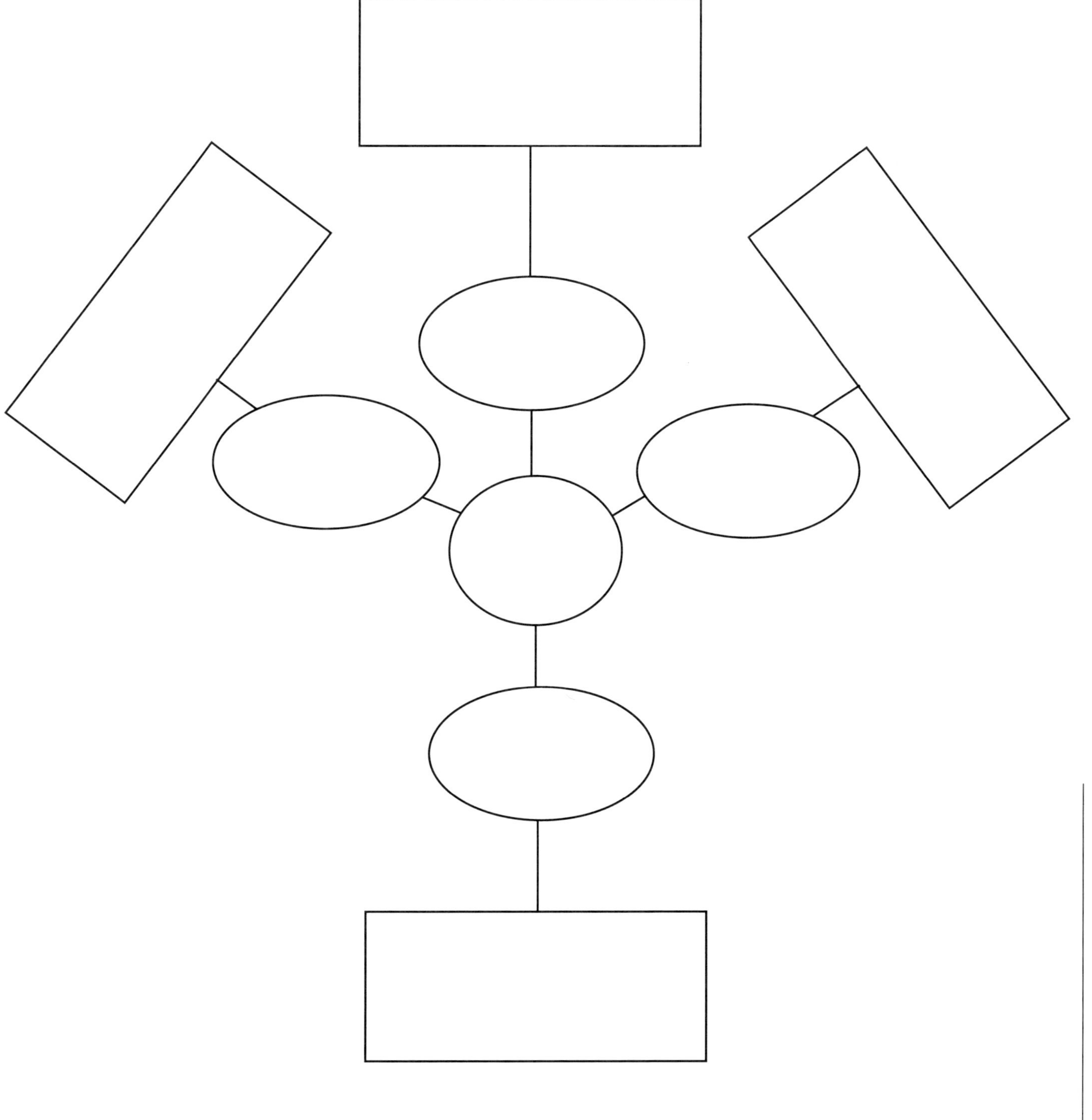

# Word Map

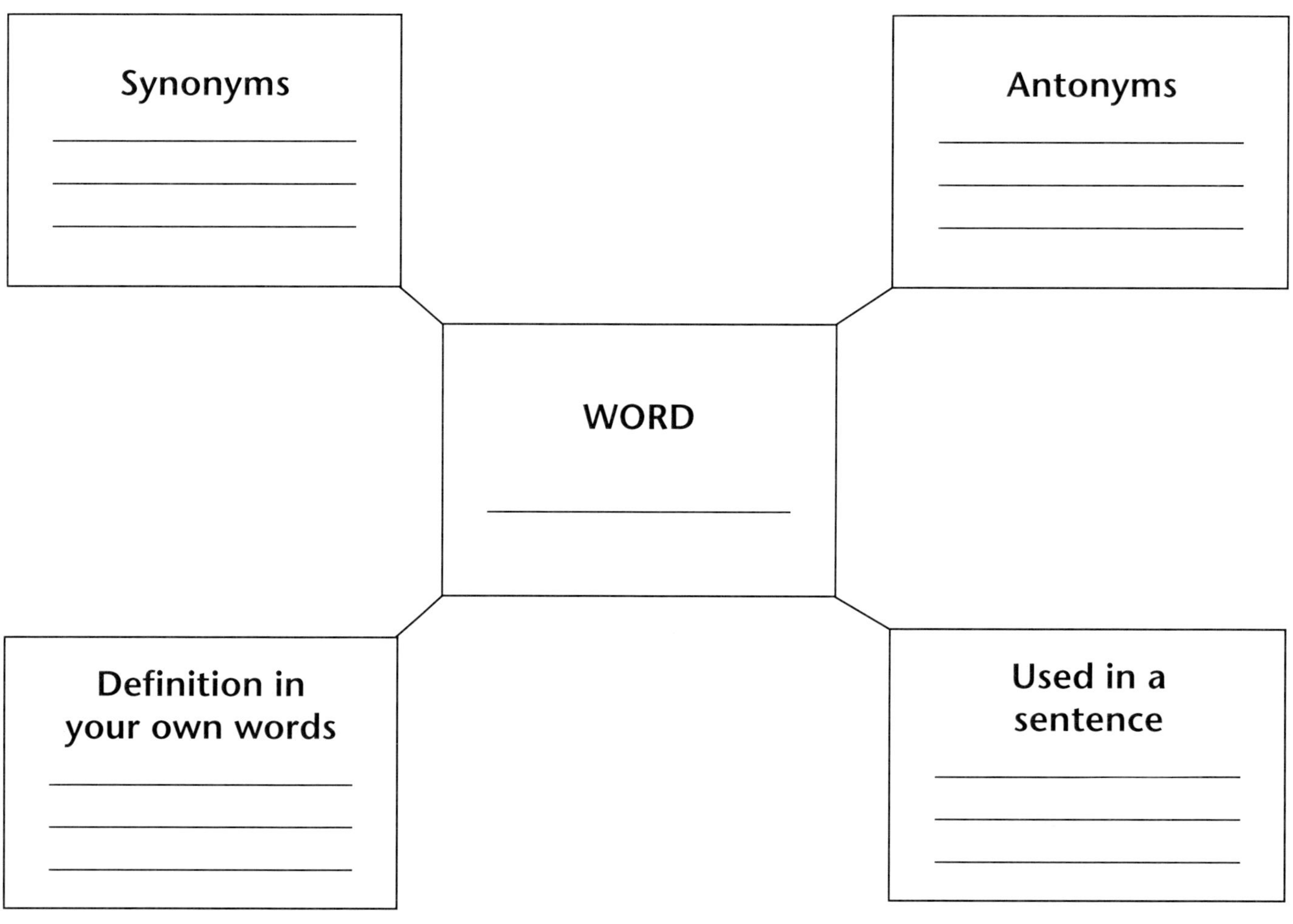




 

Synonyms
Antonyms
WORD
Definition in
your own words
Used in a
sentence

## Thought Bubble

**Directions:** In the graphic below, write what Perry may have been thinking when he read his sister's letter for the first time. Write from Perry's point of view.

# Character Analysis Blocks

**Directions:** Describe Perry Smith using the blocks below.

| *Who is the character?* |
|---|

| *What does the character do?* | *Why does he do it?* |
|---|---|

| *How does the character's family affect him?* | *What, if anything, is significant about the character's name?* | *What is the nature of this character's actions?* *(reactive, active, important, consequential, secondary)* |
|---|---|---|

| *What is the significance of the book's time and place to the character?* | *What is unusual or important about the character?* | *How does the character change in the story?* | *Does the character remind you of another character from another book? Who?* |
|---|---|---|---|

## Story Map

**Directions:** Fill in each box below with information about the book.

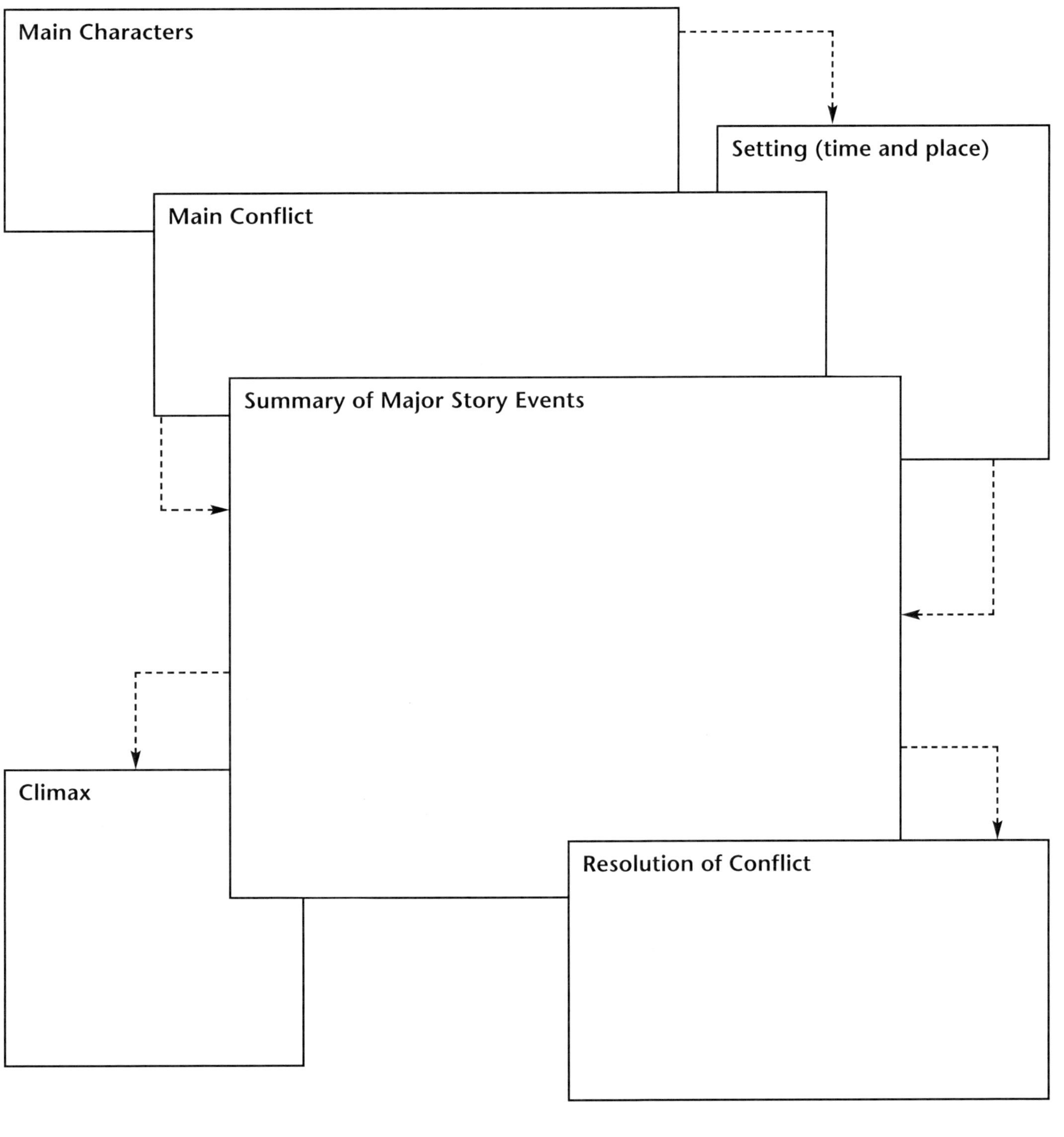

## Cause/Effect Chart

**Directions:** In the boxes below, explain the effects of Floyd Wells' discussion with Dick when they were cellmates.

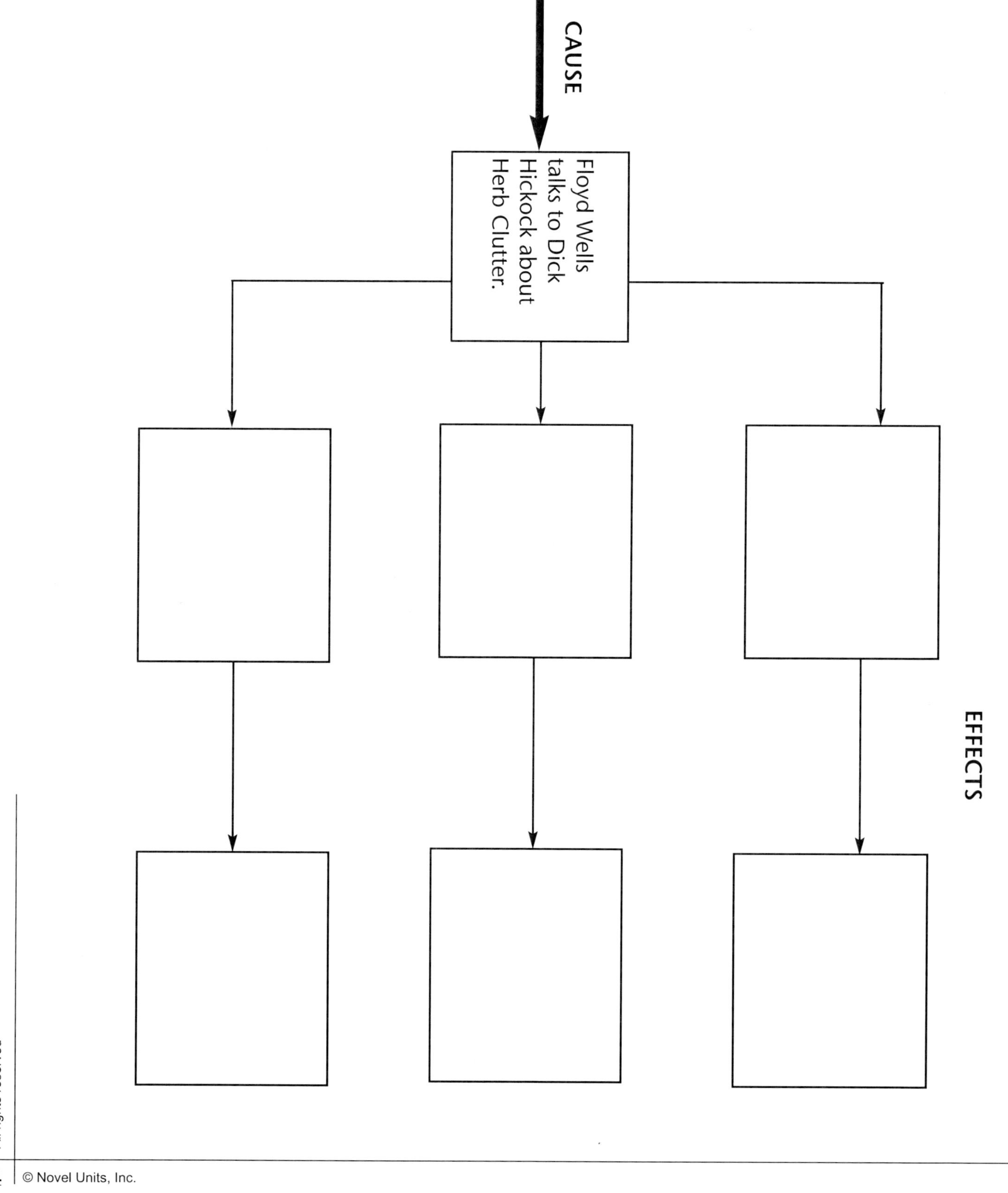

# Linking Novel Units® Lessons to National and State Reading Assessments

During the past several years, an increasing number of students have faced some form of state-mandated competency testing in reading. Many states now administer state-developed assessments to measure the skills and knowledge emphasized in their particular reading curriculum. The discussion questions and post-reading questions in this Novel Units® Teacher Guide make excellent open-ended comprehension questions and may be used throughout the daily lessons as practice activities. The rubric below provides important information for evaluating responses to open-ended comprehension questions. Teachers may also use scoring rubrics provided for their own state's competency test.

*Please note:* The Novel Units® Student Packet contains optional open-ended questions in a format similar to many national and state reading assessments.

## Scoring Rubric for Open-Ended Items

| | |
|---|---|
| **3-Exemplary** | Thorough, complete ideas/information<br>Clear organization throughout<br>Logical reasoning/conclusions<br>Thorough understanding of reading task<br>Accurate, complete response |
| **2-Sufficient** | Many relevant ideas/pieces of information<br>Clear organization throughout most of response<br>Minor problems in logical reasoning/conclusions<br>General understanding of reading task<br>Generally accurate and complete response |
| **1-Partially Sufficient** | Minimally relevant ideas/information<br>Obvious gaps in organization<br>Obvious problems in logical reasoning/conclusions<br>Minimal understanding of reading task<br>Inaccuracies/incomplete response |
| **0-Insufficient** | Irrelevant ideas/information<br>No coherent organization<br>Major problems in logical reasoning/conclusions<br>Little or no understanding of reading task<br>Generally inaccurate/incomplete response |



 

## Glossary

**Part I: The Last To See Them Alive**

**Pages 1–37**

1. haphazard: characterized by randomness
2. melancholy: gloomy; somber; causing sadness
3. exploitation: use of something, especially for profit
4. impinged: interfered with; invaded
5. disquiet: lack of calm, peace, or ease; anxiety
6. abstemious: characterized by restraint or moderation
7. despondent: feeling or showing profound hopelessness or discouragement
8. ominous: signifying evil or harm; threatening
9. mesmeric: compelling; fascinating
10. pragmatic: having a practical and realistic outlook
11. enigma: puzzling or inexplicable situation
12. reticent: reserved; reluctant to speak or act
13. ineffable: incapable of being expressed or described in words
14. elocution: study and practice of oral delivery, including the control of both voice and gesture
15. diminutive: small; little; tiny
16. vitality: exuberance; vigor; strength
17. austere: without excess or luxury; simple
18. admonition: warning; gentle reprimand
19. fastidious: excessively particular, critical, or demanding
20. truncated: shortened; cut off
21. itinerant: working in one place for a short period of time before moving on to find work in another place
22. opulent: wealthy; rich; affluent
23. wanton: deliberate and without any apparent motive

**Pages 38–74**

1. temperament: one's nature or disposition; personality
2. credulous: willing to believe or trust too readily
3. ruminations: meditations; musings; deep thoughts
4. intervene: come between, especially during a dispute; mediate
5. repertoire: stock of works a person is prepared to perform
6. agoraphobic: having a phobia (fear) of public places, crowds, and/or open spaces



 

7. anecdote: short account of a particular event or incident
8. encumbered: filled; hampered the function of
9. languid: lacking in vigor, vitality, or spirit
10. pacified: appeased; quieted; calmed
11. unassuming: acting in a way that does not display authority; modest; humble
12. varmints: despicable, obnoxious, or annoying people

**Part II: Persons Unknown**

**Pages 75–117**

1. raucous: loud; obnoxious
2. tantalized: teased and tormented by something desirous or interesting
3. abstainer: one who deliberately refrains from an action or practice
4. eccentric: different from the norm; unconventional
5. abortive: imperfectly planned or developed; unsuccessful
6. premonition: anticipation of an event without conscious reason
7. ardently: acted or spoken with passion and zealousness
8. speculations: reflections; meditations; ponderings
9. gratify: indulge; satisfy; please
10. bereaved: having suffered the death of a loved one
11. peculiarities: strange or uncommon details
12. transient: person traveling from place to place, usually in search of work
13. prolific: marked by abundant inventiveness or success

**Pages 117–155**

1. bewitched: cast a spell over; enchanted
2. prowling: moving about stealthily, usually in a predatory manner
3. purloined: stolen
4. desperado: reckless and violent (term used primarily in the southwestern United States)
5. aversion: a feeling of hatred or disgust toward something, usually accompanied by a desire to avoid it
6. incarnate: made actual or comprehensible; embodied
7. effeminate: not manly in appearance or manner; feminine
8. vagrancy: loitering without purpose or with ill intent
9. garnered: acquired; accumulated; collected
10. conventionalism: exhibiting ordinary, standard, or common ideas and behaviors

11. paradox: statement that is seemingly contradictory or opposed to common sense and yet is perhaps true
12. profundity: quality of being difficult to understand or believe
13. prognosis: conclusion; deduction
14. acquiesced: accepted or complied passively
15. pugnacity: quarrelsome or combative nature
16. sumptuous: magnificent or luxurious in appearance

**Part III: Answer**

**Pages 157–198**

1. ruination: destruction
2. ascertained: discovered or learned with certainty
3. corroborated: supported with evidence or authority
4. subdued: lacking in vitality, intensity, or strength
5. conceited: showing an excessively high opinion of oneself
6. palliatives: things that reduce the intensity of pain or disease
7. ambivalent: simultaneous and contradictory attitudes or feelings toward something or someone
8. fortitude: strength of mind; extreme courage
9. pathological: abnormal; unable to be explained
10. commodity: something useful or valued
11. permeated: spread or diffused through
12. urchin: mischievous youngster
13. cavalcade: dramatic sequence or procession
14. trivialities: things of little consequence, worth, or importance
15. delirium: frenzied excitement
16. invulnerable: incapable of being harmed

**Pages 199–248**

1. afflicted: distressed; troubled; anguished
2. reveries: wandering thoughts; daydreams
3. somnolent: sleepy; drowsy
4. succumbed: yielded to a desire
5. fervor: intensity of feeling or expression
6. circumstantial: wholly dependent on certain conditions, facts, or events; incidental
7. reconnoiter: perform a preliminary survey or observation

8. extradition: surrender of an alleged criminal by one authority to another having jurisdiction to try the charge
9. recapitulation: concise summary
10. allusions: implied or indirect references
11. sanctuary: place of refuge and protection
12. premeditation: consideration or planning beforehand that shows intent to commit a certain act
13. festooning: decorating; hanging from
14. fragmentary: incomplete; detached
15. conjectured: inferred; guessed; supposed
16. expurgated: edited to remove offensive parts; cleansed
17. fusillade: spirited outburst
18. retribution: punishment

**Part IV: The Corner**

**Pages 249–292**

1. mélange: mixture of inconsistent and/or bizarre items
2. monotonous: tediously uniform or unchanging
3. idyllic: pleasing; picturesque; simple; natural
4. stiletto: thin, pointed instrument
5. periphery: external boundary of something
6. cantankerous: difficult or irritating to deal with
7. mirthless: expressing no joy or humor
8. unpretentious: free from elegance, pride, or showiness; modest
9. odious: inspiring hatred and disgust
10. ministrations: aid or services offered by someone
11. vicissitudes: unexpected changes in fortune
12. beleaguered: troubled; harassed
13. chagrined: distressed; unsettled; humiliated
14. contrition: remorse and/or atonement for one's sins

**Pages 292–343**

1. conspicuous: obvious; attracting attention
2. predisposed: inclined to do something
3. innocuous: harmless; unlikely to offend
4. contention: point advanced or maintained in a debate or argument

5. debonair: suave; nonchalant; charming
6. perturbed: greatly disturbed or disquieted
7. callous: feeling no emotion about something; feeling no concern or sympathy for others
8. unctuous: revealing or marked by a smug, ingratiating, and false earnestness or spirituality
9. rococo: excessively ornate or intricate; flamboyant
10. uncongenial: not sympathetic or compatible
11. anathema: someone or something intensely disliked or loathed
12. pinioned: disabled or restrained by binding the arms
13. malodorous: having a bad smell, ranging from unpleasant to strongly offensive
14. progeny: descendants; children
15. prevaricate: tell a lie; mislead
16. intoned: uttered or recited in a monotone